DEAR DARWISH

DEAR DARWISH

MORANI KORNBERG-WEISS

BLAZEVOX[BOOKS]
Buffalo, New York

publisher of weird little books

BlazeVOX [books]

blazevox.org

21 20 19 18 17 16 15 14 13 12 01 02 03 04 05 06 07 08 09 10

BlazeVOX

For Guy

"I am not a prisoner of history"

– Frantz Fanon

"Your pain is the breaking
of the shell that encloses
your understanding"

– Khalil Gibran

Contents

DEAR DARWISH

Dear Mahmoud,

Dear Mahmoud Darwish,

I want to write poems about Israel and Palestine but I am at loss. What language can I use?

Jack Spicer wrote letters to the late Federico Garcia Lorca and explained that their correspondence would enable them to "use up" their rhetoric so it would not appear in their poetry. He writes, "Let it be consumed paragraph by paragraph, day by day, until nothing of it is left in it." I write to you in hopes of leaving it aside.

Mahmoud, I recently encountered these lines in a poem:
how many Arabs for each
Israeli

Mahmoud, there was another prisoner swap. An Israeli soldier held captive for five years was released in exchange for 1,027 prisoners. There were images of Palestinians who had blood on their hands and then I met J.H. and he asked me if Gilad Shalit also had blood on his hands and I wonder how many Palestinians died while he was serving in a tank. I imagine a frightened young Gilad in a deafening tank following dumb orders dumbly. We all saw photos of Aziz Salha with blood on his hands but nobody thought about the blood on Gilad's hands, myself included.

That marks one difference between Israelis and Palestinians: so many Israelis walk around with blood on their hands, hands soaked in red, red hands shaking, exchanging blood, patting a bloody hand on one's shoulder, leaving a trace of a hand, a hand running through one's hair, scratching a nose, leaving creases of liquid clotted and dried up on the cheekbones, taking a bath and then running a hand over one's arms, arm pits, breasts then thighs, genitals, feet all covered with blood, blood trying to wash itself but it's a blood so ordinary you cannot even see it.

I write this letter.

Red fingerprints smear on the page.

Mahmoud, the IDF prefers that women keep their gentle hands clean, but we are dirty.

Mahmoud, Spicer spoke of tradition as "generations of different poets in different countries patiently telling the same story, writing the same poem, gaining and losing something with each transformation – but, of course, never really losing anything."

Mahmoud, if I am an Israeli woman living in Buffalo and you reside in IsraelPalestine on my bookshelf and I read and transform your poems, are we still telling the same story? Mahmoud, do I have the right to use your words? Mahmoud, would you grant me permission to do this? Can we work together to define it and its possibilities?

האם עברית תהיה השפה המשותפת שלנו?

Should we use English?

هل يمكننا أن نستخدم اللغة العربية؟

Let me try:

You ask: "Who Am I, Without Exile?"
        (This is the title of my transformation.)

~~You are a stranger on the riverbank,~~
~~like the water... river~~
~~binds me to your name.~~
~~Nothing carries me or makes me carry an idea.~~
~~Water~~
~~binds me~~
~~to your name...~~
~~There's nothing left of you but me...~~
        (I tried stealing this from you.)

Let me try again:

"In Time of Plague"
        (I am now borrowing from Spicer.)

It "took us and the land from under us"
it soiled our hands like water:
Red stained cracks leaving
fingerprints layered with handshakes.
Red stained handles on the door

of a bus designed from the ground
upwards. Red stained water
escalating like the bricks
of demolished houses.

We have been planting
signs on the side of the road
like one thousand
bulbs under fresh earth stolen
by neighborhood squirrels.
They eat our red-stained seeds digest
the preborn and run up trees.

You ask, "Who Am I, Without Exile?" I
answer: You are the bulb of the pregrown
plant carried in the stomach
of a squirrel. You ask: Who Are You,
Without Exile? I answer: I am
wandering exile seeping my roots
in our land. You are now
the squirrel eating our bulbs snapping
water lines lifting sidewalks and we both
share the blood on our hands while I
wash them use soap and water
soap and bleach I scrub I
scrub I scrub hard until my
skin peels until I scratch the skin off
I am scrubbing my muscles and I
scrub I scrub I scrub and scrub my
bones and I scrub peel the red
peel the red peel the red until this body
becomes nothing.

I am a skeleton walking among poets.

Mahmoud,
        Please teach me how to li(v)e with these stains.

                Love,

        M

God dressed up like a soldier today
and yelled at the top of God's lungs:
"Kid, get the fuck out of there or
I'll smash your face."

There was video footage too.
A stone. A junction. A car.

One doesn't calculate the toss.

It isn't mapped out.
Or planned.

It requires a certain spontaneity.
A reaction to circumstance.

Dear Mahmoud,

I often feel like a hostage
confined to my own history.

The world is a dark room and
I am chained to the wall.

My body pressed against
cold brick loses
trace of itself.

It is stifling in here.
I can barely breathe.
The air is thick.
I taste it.

Lips damp.
Smell of excrement
and blood. Fluorescent
blubs. Electrical discharge
turned into heat. Then
the ice. Toes numb.

I starve.
I am exhausted. And when
I let my imagination
go there
I hear others.

I feel eyes on me.
The sound of smugness scorn
of satisfaction
in the corner.

Thighs attempt to remain stable.
Feet covered in urine.
Cuts burn. I try to
think
of something else.
But a voice yells.

Asks questions. And
more questions and
repeats the questions.
Demands confessions.

I can only commit to my birth:
to encountering life
at a certain point in time.

I am not responsible for this.

I try to raise a hand
to crease the limbs
lines according to their design.

A hand enters the stomach
pressing through the intestines
pushing up towards the throat
opening the mouth
moving the lips. They say:
"I did it." "It was me."

Every time I fight it
the heavy metal pushed in
dictates
every move and gesture.

The hand remains in the throat
mimicking a discourse.
"I did it." "I" "say."
It was me.

They hang
by shackles.
Low concrete wall.
Strengthen the hood.
Kick. Push. Burn. Beat
with the butt of a rifle.

The voice yells.
Asks. Questions.

The room
windowless
barely the size
of the mattress.

I say:
I am your amnesia.
The blind spot of the mid-century.

The metal confirmed on wrists
eroding into the skin
cold and cumbersome.

A body toyed with.
A pile of limbs.

Something entered here.
It hurts. I can't tell
them to stop.

This is the story
I could have told
had you unsealed my mouth.

I was born on that day.
Life, initially, is about unintention.
Possibility is frightening.

I am here because
my freedom
is terrifying and
"when people do not
want to see something
they get mad at
the one who shows them.

They kill the messenger."

Mahmoud,

    because doing this
    is exceedingly difficult

        and I should try

            to allow myself

to feel less distracted.

Let's say we put torture aside.

You know
the kind that strikes the skin.
Pries it open. Unsettles the surface.

Let's say you don't think about
the place
where those things happen.

Of having your eyelids
sewn into your cheeks
so that – God forbid – you
dare open them.

Let's say you don't allow
those thoughts to crawl
into your mind. You
keep them in a time capsule
and bury them in your backyard.

Let's say you don't see
the child's head
smash into the asphalt simply
for crying mother help stop.

Let's say that instead
you imagine sitting in a dark room.
A very dark room.

The type that forgets its own darkness
and becomes accustomed to the chaos
of small particles gliding through one another.

Let's say that in that room you
sit or perhaps stand or perhaps
your hands are tied
behind your back and now
they feel like a separate part
of your body and you can't move
them and there's a fly

that made its way to the room
and it's sitting on your cheek
and you have no way of shooing it away.

Let's say
that at some point it ceases to bother you.
You ignore its presence its existence
almost like you've learned to live
with the darkness. You breathe
shallow breaths.

You have surrendered yourself.

You say the city is thriving.
"It's never been better." That it's none of our business.
        "Don't be so naïve" you insist.
The skyscrapers are scratching the sun.
New roads paved into meadows.
High mortality rates.
Like measuring morality
with a thumb.
Press it to the wall and count the creases.
Quantify pain from zero to ten:
Zero: I have nothing to say to you.
My four is your eight.
My arm is on fire.
It started before I was born.
Look, the city is growing.
This isn't complex or subjective.
The alarming signal
is moderately unbearable.
I'm exhausted too.
The fear of pain is greater than the fear of death
and I'm confused about God.
My mind is dull clouded with burden.
The fear of knowledge is greater than the fear of pain.
God moved into that building.
God lives on the twelfth floor.
God saw the city ablaze and yelled:
"Children, behind you!"
The boy's face hit the cold stone
pavement near a holy site.
When prophets walk on this land everything is holy.
My thumb is stuck on plaster.
My pain now a two.
My two is your eight. I'm sorry
we don't feel the same way about this but God
is knocking on my door and God needs sugar.
It is early and we are going into the great nothingness.
The tender throbbing shooting in my legs
dull cutting a tight tingle.
There are many languages for this but
the truth is:
"What is mild to one person may be terrible to another."

When the Army Enters the Village

The pe pl l s
th r   ho mes.
N p ce f   ch dr n
t pl .

N p ce f r w   n
t   r   d.

N p ce f r   m n
t   p y.

N   o   c   live here   .

       (Sing:)

       No one can live here like this.
       No one can live here like this.
       No one can live here like this.

Wait. Pause. Don't put this down. Please. I know. It's painful. It hurts. I know. I do know. You don't want to hear it. You don't. I don't want to say it. I don't. I really don't. No. No. It hurts. It really hurts. It's hard. You don't want to hear it. So let's take it slow. Let's take it very slow. Real slow. Let's try to understand. Let's begin. Here is a beginning. I need you to begin. Take this beginning. I really want you to begin. Let's begin together. I know you don't want to hear it. I'm going. I see you. You are here. Let's begin. It's okay. I'm scared too. I am. Really. I'm very scared. I'm shaking. Feel me. Those are my arms. Yours. I want to feel yours. Don't be afraid. Come. Come closer. Come here. I'm scared. I'm afraid. I know you are too. This scares me. It frightens me. Let's begin. Let's get there. We should. We should try. We must try. We must get there.

Dear Mahmoud,

Once it starts it cannot stop:
It slowly creeps into you
like a small insect burrowing
through your palm sluggishly
shifting towards your elbow
passing your heart
and invading your brain.

Mahmoud,
I have been living with this creature for some time.

The minute it entered my body
I departed from my self.

I am no incidental host.

Mahmoud,
This is living.

The antennas sulk into cardboard
assemble their feeble bodies to fit
interlocking pieces: a game of war.
Her body will not center. She will vomit
until the insides devour the image she
held onto. She hovered low for too long
and now becomes the cocoon mouthed in a leaf:
Fly blind one. Embrace your legs and wings.
You are a form of misunderstanding
not a carrier of disease but
nocturnal. Awaiting
more spectacular migrations.

We are bound in this eternity:
The present moment negating its own borders
and boundaries. You and I walk circular
and tall. We are contained in endless mirrors.
It is only our own miseries we see.

I often imagine every Israeli and every Palestinian
wearing cylindrical masks without eyeholes
bumping into the same recollection. Mahmoud,
I must shatter them: a simultaneous circumcision.

What if
we all climb
the mountain
and sacrifice
our masks while
the hand of God
remains still
and we cut the skins
of ourselves peeling
layer after layer
until we obliterate all
remembrance?

Imagine a mass circumcision
of our bodies men women and children
skeletal without sustaining
a past but despite themselves
allowing questions to evaporate
into another existence.

Some times
I am sutured
loosely but exposed
like a paper cut.

Unhealed.
Open.
A scar-reskinning.

It began
with a small shift.
A sever.

Quiet like an earthquake.

You and I meet on the borders
of language where words
encounter the objects
they are designed to signify.

I cannot locate you anywhere.

You are the place
where language fails
and I am the translator
of no language.

I must internalize you
so we become nothing other.

You and I cannot
demand the future
but only our presence.

Here
you insist on my hand
settling in its place
cradling the other
reaching only for a pen.

"We cannot rid ourselves of the form
to which we now belong"

– Robert Duncan

There.

I put you in this poem:

<   >

Now
you I we together
in this poem.

You might think it strange
might not want to be here
but it is now a fact:

We are now in this poem.

The space
we share
it: see:

I you I you I you I you

What if I stand above you
(in this poem):

I
You

Would you think it strange?

What if you
stand above me?

You
me

or:

You
I

I don't know how to share
this poem with you.

I don't know how to put you
in this poem
but I don't think it strange.

What's strange
is you
are so close
and so abruptly far

and this poem
is ours.

dear mahmoud,

david antin talked about tuning and about how

"i was
beginning to arrive at the notion
of how far we might be
from each other and what
sort of distance
we might have to travel"

"i would
like to contribute to human not understanding" mahmoud "i
would like to slow down" to learn how to not understand so you
and i are not so foreign so you and i break away
from the "fantasy of understanding"

i barely
recognize myself in you mahmoud i
recount various experiences of misappropriation i
imagine no common knowing but my arrogant
fantasy of moving so close in you mahmoud
so close you and i do not recognize each other
and act politely like strangers do

what a fantasy
for understanding mahmoud no preconceptions
no knowledge imagine this frame of mind imagine
no common knowing of the always
possible not knowing:

a deep conflict
where we decide if we got lost or lost ourselves

from an m

"I have woven a parachute out
of everything broken; my scars
are my shield"

– William Stafford

Dear Mahmoud,

I want to fall into the dark sky
night and deadly. You would
hold my hand carry
me away from burden become
the fear in my chest that keeps me
awake and alert. I would never
feel alone: you would follow me
carry my body light like water
settle the space where the skin
becomes weightless.

We'd be greater than the Mediterranean.

I am the feather on your lips
puny and minute.
You are the remembrance
throbbing in my chest
the type that races
the heart and occupies the throat
so I become thirsty of you.

Dear Mahmoud:

I lay naked tired crumpled up: the usual mess.
I don't want this one to be political Mahmoud.

So it won't be:

I undo you:
In the presence of your absence
I begin to remove the pages of you
one by one:

You "come" "into this merciless night"
a "rendezvous" "promised"
in a "glass of red wine."
Mahmoud, "I would have possessed you,
and had you known me,
you would have possessed me."
And "then you and I" "would"
become "rhythmic collusion."

Mahmoud, I "lie stretched
out before" you.
"This does not keep us
from recalling" our "love."
You and I now create
a "private tomorrow"
"a tale of two travelers"
"who never parted company."

It is day in here.
The room stands, bed
upright, I, another crease
in the sheets. The dimness
of morning, a cat mounted
on the night stand
and your words.

I undo you
letter by letter
breaking apart lines:

"They say: where is the proof?"
I return: "where is the truth?"

It is early Mahmoud.
I toss over
my hand bracing my thigh
and then: involuntary action:

The pages smooth
in my hand uneven
made stiff. A rigid
living breathing object.

I make hundreds
of balls of you:
Placing each page in my hand
before crushing them into
structural complexity.

You are now most dense
in your outer regions.

I move you into my mouth
place your letters among my teeth
and swallow each line.
Then elaborately pulp
the pieces into one
and push you in.

"The poem is incomplete."

It moves in my body
and "my question wakes you up"
caressing my thighs.

Good morning.

Dear Mahmoud,

I want you to know my daily morning routine:
Wake up. Snooze. Five minutes. Five more. Get out of bed.
Urinate. Extend hand. Soap. Open faucet. Wash hands. Face.

Then

without speaking or thinking or interacting:
I pour water from the Brita into the kettle and switch it on.
I select a coffee mug from the cabinet
pour two teaspoons of coffee one teaspoon of sugar

and wait.

I accomplish many things during this time of waiting:

I water the plants or clean the cats' litter box or feed the dog or
select a dress or wash a few dishes or quickly answer an email or
wait patiently for the water to boil or check the mail or let the
dog out or fold another shirt or listen or watch the birds or stare
blankly or think and on occasion I run up and put on my
makeup because it often takes less than two minutes to put on
face cream foundation eye shadow and mascara – but never
lipstick – because there is coffee to drink and I don't want to
stain the cup.

Mahmoud, there are times when I read the news and when I sit
and write and tire the coffee until it's too cold to drink.

But never, never Mahmoud
do I prefer makeup over coffee
and always,
always Mahmoud
always is the insistence of obsession
the longing for
sweeter bitterness
in my mouth.

Yours,
M

Dear Mahmoud,

Many poems are
dedicated
to other writers.
The indication: a "for."

I wonder about these offerings.
Do they begin with the addressee in mind
or does the gift-receiver appear midway?

Mahmoud, these letters
are not "for" you.
They are *to* you:
A direct bearing
without mediation.
A movement towards.
A form of contact
and proximity.
A relative position.
A purpose.
An intention.
A process.
A response.

A form of belonging.

Mahmoud, Spicer writes: "In the white endlessness
                        How pure and big a wound
                        His imagination left."

Spicer had Lorca "respond:"
"He" "said," "'The dead are notoriously hard to satisfy.'"
Spicer later adds, "the dead are very patient."

Mahmoud, I am testing this patience of yours.
I would like to see where it takes us.

For now: our wounds shift
their edges into the center
formulating a perfectly

symmetrical square
without the remnants
of cheap mass-produced pulps.
I am creating the envelope.

Ours remains a one-way correspondence.

An addressee without an address.

I refuse to colonize you.

Yours,
M

"The echo has no echo
so she becomes the endless scream:"

Her voice is a disturbance
with no permanent displacement.

What matters is how she
proceeds over time:

Her house falling under a bomb.
"The sea is a warship having fun."

She lay between a point within chaos
and a moment of comprehension.

Where logics cancel each other out.

Her phase changes slowly
and reverberates in harmonic motion.

The scene: an exhibition of diffraction.
        "'The sea is not for people like us!'"

Neither is the land.

That anger there
sitting packed up
neatly on a Monday night.

These tears are filth.
Those are just memories.
Someone's testimony.

A distilled truth.

The placemats look like flags.
Repetition within production.

She cannot orchestrate the past.
It just happened.

A monotonous ending
in a tattoo made of numbers.

We must learn to read
ink so five soldiers disallow
dogs from eating
breasts like canned food.

Plan D

To erase
is to acknowledge
that one is
and must no longer be.

To erase
an individual
is to efface
and dispossess.

To erase
a village
is a futile attempt
to relocate.

The remains cannot be moved
even with the strongest force.

To erase
a people
is to ignore
that demolition

can never
cleanse
history.

סְלִיחָה

What was once seen
from here
is a house.

A body with four
walls now
succumbs
to the ground.

When walls fall
like limbs

bodies become
houses.

סְלִיחָה

When walls fall
limbs are houses.

סְלִיחָה

Nobody lived in that house.

סְלִיחָה

The morning paper
reported:

no body
occupied that house.

סְלִיחָה

The walls fall on their
bodies
relieving our tension.

It wasn't us.

It was the house.

Houses guarantee
bodies return
to the ground.

סְלִיחָה

After *Yom Kippur*

Dear Mahmoud,

Tonight I will repent for all my sins.

I am about to beg for forgiveness for my sins.
I am about to pray.
I am just about to seek forgiveness and

atone for my wrongdoings.

I will ask that my sins be absolved.
I am about to amend my behavior.
I will beg to be forgiven for my sins
against other human beings:

I shall bathe my flesh in water
And come forth
And make atonement for myself.
I shall afflict my soul.
For this day shall atonement be made
for me, to cleanse me
from all my sins.
And this shall be an everlasting statue unto me.

Mahmoud,

> I will remove my clothes my socks and my shoes. I will
> walk to the bathroom and open the faucet move my face
> beneath the water and slowly begin to remove my
> makeup.

> I will not eat or drink.

> I will stand before you utterly undone:

> Tonight is the night of atonement, and I am about to
> repent for my sins.

> Mahmoud, tonight I am about to beg for forgiveness.

I will stand naked before you until my soul cracks, and I
atone for my wrongdoings.

I am about to afflict my soul.
I am about to demonstrate my repentance.
I will make amends before the book is sealed.
I will stand before you completely whole.
I will record my misdoings my crimes and confess:

אָשַׁמְנוּ, בָּגַדְנוּ,	We abominated. Beat.
גָּזַלְנוּ, דִּבַּרְנוּ דֹּ פִי,	Captivated. Cleansed. Demolished.
הֶעֱוִינוּ, וְהִרְשַׁעְנוּ, זַדְנוּ,	Displaced. Effaced. Exiled. Fought.
חָמַסְנוּ, טָפַלְנוּ שֶׁקֶר, יָעַצְנוּ רָע,	Gated. Hated. Isolated. Jeopardized.
כִּזַּבְנוּ, לַצְנוּ, מָרַדְנוּ,	Killed. Labored. Murdered. Neglected.
	Occupied. Oppressed. Policed.
נִאַצְנוּ, סָרַרְנוּ, עָוִינוּ,	Quarreled. Raped. Sentenced.
פָּשַׁעְנוּ, צָרַרְנוּ, קִשִּׁינוּ עֹ רֶף,	Silenced. Suppressed.
רָשַׁעְנוּ,שִׁחַתְנוּ, תִּעַבְנוּ,	Tortured. Uprooted. Violated.
תָּעִינוּ, תִּעְתָּעְנוּ	Wronged. X-ed. Yanked. Zoned.

Mahmoud,
I have intentionally sinned,
I have sinned out of lust and emotion,
and I have sinned unintentionally.

Mahmoud, *before I was formed I was worthless*
and now that I am formed I am as if not formed.

Mahmoud, I am about to remit my errors.
I will ask to be pardoned.
I will absolve my shame and disgrace.

Mahmoud, tonight I will stand before you.

Just my soul
open and ablaze:

Dear Mahmoud,

      I

I think you should know that I

      I am trying really hard   I
        I

I am struggling.

      I want to know   I

I do not know what this should look like

  I
I am   I am   , I

      I need to know,

         I
I want to learn   I'm
    I   I want to   I

      , here Mahmoud

           I need   I

    It is difficult,   I

Love,
أنا

Dear Mahmoud,

I'm trying to collect words
like seashells on the shore.
I would like to hang them
in my poems as ornaments
so window-shoppers can stop
by and purchase every syllable.

See what I have collected
from this language!

"As if a word could
become an object
by mere addition
of consequences."

The line remains unsatisfactory.
The spaces between them too deep.
I can place a fingernail among two
and examine the blue ink
touch the tip of my skin.

I walk away from the page
and soft ashes shed off
my hand: the world creased
within every line of my palm
and still –

you are dead.

And still –
the people are sleepy
like dried flowers pressed
into the skeleton of the sky.
A word turning the world.
A word gesturing towards another:

In this I can see how weak
poetry really is. How it can
only take me as far
as you will let me go.

Yours, truly,
M

Reclaiming Space

The concern
for liberation
and bodily
containment
reaffirms
the borders:

One draws lines
names states
excludes
exiles
imagines and

mobility
is what we
now call
practice.

One state
two states
three states four.

Five states
six states
seven galore!

Eight states
nine states ten
states too.

Aren't we tired,
me and you?

After November 29

Today I stand before you tall and proud.

I stand as *a nation with deep roots in the past*

and bright hopes for the future.

Today *I stand before you* and tell you:
I *never hesitate* to *defend* myself. But
I *will always extend* my *hand for peace.*

I seek peace. I pursue peace.

I always look for peace
reach out for peace
extend my hand for peace.

Peace is a central value of my *society. The bible calls on us:*
"seek peace and pursue it."

סוּר מֵרָע, וַעֲשֵׂה טוֹב;   Depart from evil, and do good;
בַּקֵּשׁ שָׁלוֹם וְרָדְפֵהוּ   seek peace and pursue it.

I mean:

Depart from evil, and do good;
seek peace and pursue it.
(or more accurately:)

רְדֹף   seek peace and chase it;
רְדֹף   seek peace and haunt it;
רְדֹף   seek peace and trouble it;
רְדֹף   seek peace and oppress it;
רְדֹף   seek peace and persecute it.

You come before me
at a time when
you are *still tending*
your *wounds*
and still burying
your *beloved*
martyrs

of children, women and men
who have fallen victim
to the latest of my aggression,
still searching for
remnants of life
amid the ruins of homes
destroyed by my bombs,
wiping out entire families,
their men, women and children
murdered
along with their dreams,
their hopes, their future
and their longing
to live
an ordinary life
and to live in freedom
and peace.

You tell me you believe *in peace*
because your *people*
are in desperate need of it.

I *know* you are in desperate need of it, but
I need to you recognize me.
I want you to recognize me.

Say it.
Say that you recognize me.

Confirm my legitimacy.
I am not legitimate without
your confirmation and without
your confirmation
I cannot confirm you.

You see,
my *security must be protected.*
You *must recognize* me
and you *must*
be prepared
to end

the conflict
with me
once
and for all.

You see, *none of these vital interests, these vital interests of peace,*

(these vital interests of peace that you just came to *reaffirm*
through your *presence* by *trying to protect the possibilities and the
foundations of a just peace that is deeply hoped for because* your
people, as proven in past days, are in desperate need)

None of these vital interests of peace
appear in the resolution that you *put forward*

                    and that is why I cannot accept it.

This resolution is so one-sided:
It doesn't advance peace:
It pushes it backwards.

My security and national interests are being ignored.

You speak of my
        aggression against your *people.*
        Of the *urgent and pressing need*
        to end
        my *occupation*
        and for your *people*
        to gain their freedom and
        independence.

You mention that I adhere
        to the policy of occupation, brute force and war. But

                Peace is a central value of my society:
                Peace fills my art and poetry.
                It is taught in my schools.
                It has been the goal of my people.

The bible says I must seek peace and oppress.

You *say with great pain and sorrow*
there was certainly no one in the world
that required that tens of
children lose their lives
in order to reaffirm
the above-mentioned facts.

There was no need
for thousands of deadly raids
and tons of explosives
for the world to be reminded
that there is an occupation
that must come to an end and
that there are a people
that must be liberated.

And, there was no need for a new, devastating war
in order for us to be aware of the absence of peace.

But my people have ties to this land.

I have a simple message for you:
no decision can break the 4000 year old bond
between my *people*
and the land.

You speak of your people
who miraculously recovered from the ashes
intended to extinguish their being
and to expel them
in order to uproot
and erase their presence
which was rooted
in the depths
of their land and depths
of history.

You mention how people were
>   *torn from their homes*
>   *and displaced*
>   *within and outside of their*
>   *homeland*
>   *thrown from their beautiful, embracing, prosperous*
>   *country*
>   *to refugee camps*
>   *in one of the most dreadful campaigns of*
>   *ethnic cleansing*
>   *and dispossession*
>   *in modern history.*

You talk of how your ***people***
>   *have strived not to*
>   *lose their humanity*
>   *their highest, deeply-held*
>   *moral values*
>   *and their innovative*
>   *abilities for*
>   *survival,*
>   *steadfastness,*
>   *creativity and hope*
>   *despite*
>   *the horrors*
>   *that befell them*
>   *and continue*
>   *to befall them*

>   ***today***

>   *as a consequence of*
>   my ***horrors***.

But *peace can only be achieved through negotiations*
by recognizing me.

I wait for you to admit *that peace*
must also address my *security needs*

>   *and end the conflict once and for all.*

You prefer *symbolism over reality*.

You would *travel to New York*
rather than travel to Jerusalem
for genuine dialogue.

> (Because I have been listening.)

You see, I *always extend* my *hand for peace and will always extend* my
hand for peace.

> (I am listening.)

I want *good neighborliness* and *to establish bonds of cooperation and*
mutual help.

> (I am listening.)

When I face a *leader who* wants *peace,* I make *peace.*

> (I am listening.)

Time and again, I *have sought peace with* you.

> (I am listening.)

> *Time and again,* I *have been met by rejection of* my *offers*
> *denial of* my *rights, and terrorism targeting* my *citizens.*

(You mention the **children, women and men**
who have fallen victim to the latest of my *aggression*
still searching for remnants of life amid the ruins of homes
destroyed by my *bombs.* You claim that I wipe *out entire*
families, men, women and children murdered.) But
I *always extend* my *hand for peace.*

You claim:

> **Despite the enormity and weight of this task,** you have
> **consistently strived to achieve harmony and conformity.**
> You have made a **historic, difficult and courageous**
> **decision that defined the requirements for a historic**
> **reconciliation that would turn the page on war, aggression**
> **and occupation.**

You describe today as
"historic."

*But the only thing historic
about your speech is how much
it ignores history.*

*The truth is:
partition:
two states:
two states for two peoples.*

I *accept this plan.*
You *reject it and
launch a war of
annihilation
to throw* us *into the sea.*

You state:
> *This was not an easy matter.*
> And:
> We *have surely witnessed how
> some of these threats
> have been carried out
> in a barbaric and horrific manner.*

> You mention that you *have not
> heard one word from* me *expressing
> any sincere concern
> to save
> the peace process.*

> *On the contrary,* you *have witnessed,
> and continue to witness,
> an unprecedented intensification
> of military assaults,
> the blockade, settlement activities and
> ethnic cleansing,
> and mass arrests, attacks by settlers
> and other practices by which
> this occupation*

is becoming synonymous with
an apartheid system
of colonial occupation,
which institutionalizes the plague of
racism
and entrenches
hatred
and incitement.

But, the truth is, *the truth is that*
you sought my destruction.

The truth is that
I made far-reaching offers for peace.
Those offers were met by rejection, evasion, and even terrorism.

The truth is that
to advance peace,
I dismantle entire communities and
uproot thousands of people from their homes.

And rather than use this opportunity to build a peaceful future,
you *refuse to accept responsibility.*
You *refuse to make the tough decisions for peace.*

I remain *committed to peace, but*

You blame me for
my ***aggressive policies and the perpetration***
of war crimes
because you think
that I think that
I am ***above the law***
and have ***immunity***
from accountability
and consequences.

(This belief is bolstered by the failure by some to condemn
and demand the cessation of its violations and crimes and
by position that equate the victim and the executioner.)

I want to disarm you. To *ensure a secure future for* myself.

That's right.

I want you *demilitarized*. I want you to *recognize* me.

That's right.

I want you disarmed vulnerable weak defenseless unprotected unguarded demilitarized.

That's right.

I want you open and exposed and dependent.

That's right.

Because you *never recognize* me.
You *have never been willing to accept.*

In fact, today you ask the world to recognize you,
but you still refuse to recognize me.

You don't recognize me. You say:

> "I *did not come here seeking to delegitimize a State*
> *established years ago; rather*
> I *came to affirm the legitimacy of the State that must now*
> *achieve its independence.*
> I *did not come here to add further complications to the*
> *peace process, which* your *policies have thrown into the*
> *intensive care unit; rather*
> I *came to launch a final serious attempt to achieve peace.*
> My *endeavor is not aimed at terminating what remains of*
> *the negotiations process,*
> *which has lost its objective and credibility, but rather*
> *aimed at trying to breathe new life*
> *into the negotiations and at setting*
> *a solid foundation."*

You *never recognize* me.

You *have never been willing to accept. In fact, today you ask the world to recognize* you, *but you still refuse to recognize* me. You say, "I *did not come here seeking to delegitimize a State established years ago; rather* I *came to affirm the legitimacy of the State that must now achieve its independence.*"

Not only do you not recognize me, you are also trying to erase my history.

You *say:*   "I *will not give up*
                 I *will not tire*
                 and my *determination will not wane*
                 and I *will continue to strive to achieve a just peace.*"

You believe that your *people will not relinquish their inalienable national rights.*
And your *people cling*
to the right
to defend themselves
against aggression and occupation and
they will continue their popular, peaceful resistance and
their epic steadfastness and
will continue to build on their land.
And, they will end the division and
strengthen their national unity.
You *will accept no less than*

                                        independence
                                        to live in peace and security
                                        alongside me.

You see, *peace*
fills my *art and*
                 poetry.

70

Peace is a central value of my *society. The bible calls on us:*

> *"'seek peace and pursue it.'"*

I want you to recognize me.
Because I seek peace. I pursue peace.

I always look for peace
reach out for peace
extend my hand for peace.

> You say that *we must repeat*
> *here once again our warning:*
> *the window of opportunity is narrowing*
> *and time is quickly running out.*
>
> *The rope of patience is shortening*
> *and hope is withering.*
>
> *The innocent lives that have been taken*
> *are a painful reminder to the world that this*
> *racist,*
> *colonial*
> *occupation*
> *is making the prospect for realizing*
> *peace*
> *a very difficult*
> *choice,*
> *if not*
> *impossible.*

You insist:

> *It is time for action*
> *and the moment to*
> *move forward.*

I believe that *instead of revising history*

> (instead of
> revising

history,
which I
erase
cleanse
destroy
rewrite)

it is time that you start
making history
by making peace.

You ask *the world to undertake a significant step*
in the process of rectifying the unprecedented
historical injustice.
You want *every voice,*
every *valuable voice*
of courage
to *support* you.

You want affirmation
of *principled and moral support*
for freedom
and the rights of peoples
and international law and peace.

You want *a promising message – to millions*
in the refugee camps both in the homeland and the
Diaspora, and to the prisoners struggling for freedom –
that justice is possible and that there is a reason
to be hopeful and that the peoples of the world
do not accept the continuation of the occupation.

But

This resolution will not advance peace.
This resolution will not change the situation on the ground.
You can't even visit nearly half the territory of the state you claim to
represent.

You can't visit nearly half the territory of the state you claim to represent because I have placed laws roadblocks entire cities schools homes municipalities parks army bases security cameras shopping malls surveillance watchtowers pavements concrete metal detectors checkpoints turnstiles segregated roads military patrols settler militia checkpoints and walls and settlements and walls and settlements and walls and settlements and checkpoints and walls and settlements and walls and settlements and checkpoints and walls and settlements and walls and settlements and checkpoints and walls and settlements and walls and settlements and walls and settlements and checkpoints and walls and settlements and checkpoints and walls and settlements and walls and walls between you and the territory of the state you claim to represent. So *you can't even visit nearly half the territory of the state you claim to represent.*

You want *support*
and *a reason for hope*
to a people besieged by a racist,
colonial occupation.
You want your *people* to know
that they are not alone.

But your *resolution*
– to be independent
to be free of occupation
to have hope –
clearly fails to meet the criteria for statehood.
This resolution cannot serve as acceptable
terms of reference for peace negotiations.
Because this resolution says nothing about
my *security needs.*

Let me tell you what this resolution does do:

This resolution violates a fundamental
binding commitment.
This is a commitment that many of the states here
were themselves witness to.
It was a commitment that all outstanding issues
in the peace process
would only be resolved
in direct negotiations.

We have tried direct negotiations
and they fail because I
want you
demilitarized
and vulnerable.

We have tried direct negotiations
but I cannot let go.
I cannot let you go.

I want to sustain this stagnation.

You *will always adhere to international humanitarian
law, uphold equality, guarantee civil liberties, uphold the
rule of law, promote democracy and pluralism, and uphold
and protect the rights of women.*

But

You are *willing to turn a blind eye to peace agreements.*
Why continue to make painful sacrifices for peace,
in exchange for pieces of paper that the other side will not honor?

You *continue to harden* your *position*
and place further obstacles and preconditions
to negotiations and peace.
And unfortunately, it will raise expectations
that cannot be met,
which has always proven
to be a recipe for conflict and instability.

There are no shortcuts.

No quick fixes.

No instant solutions.

> You see,
> there are walls and settlements
> and imprisonments and laws
> and soldiers and roadblocks
> and cities and checkpoints
> and walls and settlements
> and walls and settlements
> and walls and settlements
> and more walls
> and more settlements. *That's right.*

"Peace cannot be imposed from the outside"
but occupation can be.
Settlements can be imposed
from the outside.
Roadblocks and checkpoints
and laws can be imposed
from the outside.
But peace? Peace!
Peace cannot be imposed
from the outside.

In submitting this resolution,
you are *once again making the wrong choice.*
You *could have chosen to live side-by-side with* me.

> (Do you remember that?
> Remember when I expelled you
> from your home?
> I didn't let you
> return to your home.
> Why didn't you accept half of it then?
> Why did you refuse
> to share

more than half with me?
After I demolish your home
expel you from your land
kill
your men, women, and children
rape
and murder
exile
and demolish
destroy your vegetation
destroy your livestock
destroy your villages
destroy your people
destroy possibilities for peace

Why didn't you *choose* then?)

You *could have chosen to accept*
the solution of two states for two peoples.
You *rejected it then, and*
you *are rejecting it again today.*

(You are whispering. I can barely make
   out a word.

Are you speaking? Are you saying you
will act responsibly and positively in your
next steps, and will to work to strengthen
cooperation with the countries and peoples
of the world for the sake of a just peace?

Are you speaking?)

You are driving *recklessly*
with both feet pressing down on the gas,
no hands on the wheel,
and no eyes on the road.

You should *enter into direct negotiations*
without preconditions

in order to achieve an historic peace
in which you remain *demilitarized* and
recognize me in all my military might.

   The truth is that I *want peace, and* you *are avoiding peace.*

You *are turning* your *back on peace.*

Don't let history record that today
you were *helped along on* your *march of folly.*

You now draw on my birth,
recall the inauguration of my **birth certificate**.

   You ask me to stand
   before a moral duty,
   which I *must not hesitate to undertake,*
   and stand before a historic duty,
   which cannot endure further delay,
   and before a practical duty
   to salvage the chances for peace,
   which is urgent
   and cannot
   be postponed.

   You want *to issue a birth certificate.*

I can barely make out your words:

       The moment....

               has arrived....

       for the world.......

               to say clearly...

Enough
aggression
settlements
occupation.

Enough
aggression
settlements
occupation.

This is why we are here now.

This is why
in specific
we are here today.

Nakba Museum

"There is a direct relationship between the force of that suffering and the place of the peoples in the human struggle for progress"

— Emile Habiby,
"Your Holocaust, Our Catastrophe"

Not claims of memory
Nor public affirmations
Not narratives of the past
Nor struggles against a much contested present
Not confrontations with dominant discourses
Nor demarcations of lines between two opposing periods
Not erasures of stories
Nor creations of baselines
Not businesses for sorting generations
Nor to publicize personal memories
Not creations of authoritative histories
Nor depositories of traces or methods for
binding states and nations
Not memories made public
Nor the embodiment of displacement
Not apparatuses of historical production
Nor the need for witnesses or empathic listeners or audiences,
otherwise stories are annihilated
Not the production of memories under constant threat of
obliteration
Nor storage houses with artifacts
And absolutely no archives or categorically collected containers
of what counts as
historical truth

We must speak counter-histories "or equivocation will undo us"

I am searching for a Nakba museum
I would very much like to visit a Nakba museum
I wonder how I would get to a Nakba museum
I am curious about the opening hours and admission fees of a
Nakba museum
I wonder if I can get a student discount at a Nakba Museum
I am interested in seeing new exhibitions at a Nakba museum
I would really like to take a guided tour at a Nakba museum
I am curious about volunteering at a Nakba Museum
I wonder if they need someone to translate texts from Hebrew to
English at a Nakba museum
I also love gift shops and hope there's one at a Nakba museum

I would have to plan a trip around the world in order to visit every Holocaust Museum, education center, and memorial:

Buenos Aires, Argentina
Melbourne, Victoria, Australia
Sydney, New South Wales, Australia
Mauthausen, Austria
Vienna, Austria
Minsk, Belarus
Mechelen, Belgium
São Paulo, Brazil
Sofia, Bulgaria
Montreal, Canada
Toronto, Canada
Vancouver, Canada
Jasenovac, Croatia
Jägala, Estonia
Klooga, Estonia
Agen, France
Angoulême, France
Anterrieux, France
Arles, France
Besançon, France
Blois, France
Bondues, France
Bordeaux, France
Bourges, France
Brive-la-Gaillarde, France
Caen, France
Castellane, France
Castelnau-le-Lez, France
Châlons-en-Champagne, France
Chamalières, France
Champigny-sur-Marne, France
Châteaubriant, France
Colombey-les-Deux-Églises, France
Compiègne, France
Fargniers, France
Forges-les-Eaux, France
Frugières-le-Pin, France
Grenoble, France
Izieu, France
La Balme-de-Thuy, France

Lorris, France
Lyon, France
Montauban, France
Montluçon, France
Montreuil, France
Nantua, France
Neuvic, France
Nice, France
Oradour-sur-Glane, France
Paris, France
Peyrat-le-Château, France
Reims, France
Rimont, France
Romans-sur-Isère, France
Saint-Brisson, France
Saint-Étienne, France
Saint-Marcel, France
Natzwiller, France
Tarbes, France
Tergnier, France
Thouars, France
Toulouse, France
Varennes-Vauzelles, France
Varilhes, France
Vassieux-en-Vercors, France
Villargondran, France
Berlin, Germany
Soest, Germany
Athens, Greece
Budapest, Hungary
Jerusalem, Israel
Tel-Yizhaq, Israel
Yad Mordechai, Israel
Western Galilee, Israel
Prato, Italy
Rome, Italy
Torino, Italy
Kaiserwald, Latvia
Rumbula, Latvia
Salaspils, Latvia
Skopje, Macedonia
Amsterdam, Netherlands

Bełżec, Poland
Łódź, Poland
Oświęcim, Poland
Treblinka, Poland
Warsaw, Poland
Cape Town, South Africa
Durban, South Africa
Johannesburg, South Africa
Stockholm, Sweden
Nottinghamshire, England, U.K.
London, England, U.K.
Chandler, Arizona, U.S.
Los Angeles, California, U.S.
Palm Desert, California, U.S.
San Francisco, California, U.S.
Washington, D.C., U.S.
Miami Beach, Florida, U.S.
St. Petersburg, Florida, U.S.
Kennesaw, Georgia, U.S.
Atlanta, Georgia, U.S.
Skokie, Illinois, U.S.
Terre Haute, Indiana, U.S.
Baltimore, Maryland, U.S.
Boston, Massachusetts, U.S.
Detroit, Michigan, U.S.
Lincoln, Nebraska, U.S.
Jersey City, New Jersey, U.S.
Albuquerque, New Mexico, U.S.
New York, New York, U.S.
Portland, Oregon, U.S.
Harrisburg, Pennsylvania, U.S.
Philadelphia, Pennsylvania, U.S.
Whitwell, Tennessee, U.S.
Dallas, Texas, U.S.
El Paso, Texas, U.S.
Houston, Texas, U.S.
San Antonio, Texas, U.S.
Richmond, Virginia, U.S.
Milwaukee, Wisconsin, U.S.

I recall visiting a Holocaust museum.
Perhaps *Yad Vashem*.

I often fail to remember the numerous details of this visit but:

> The tribute to children. The reflection of
> candlelight and their names overheard in the
> backdrop of immense darkness. Walking through
> mirrors. Seeing only one tiny light expand
> infinitely.

Being blinded by the heat once I step out. I might
have made my way back in. I am almost positive I
did. I wanted to stay there for a while. As if my
presence might enhance the act of remembering
and in my remembrance the children lived
through me.

Or lived somehow.

I recall this visit.

I was with my parents.
My mother kept on saying how
sad it is.

There

    I confronted the landscape of Jerusalem.
    It startled me in its sadness.

I am still searching for a Nakba Museum.

    I check online.
    I don't find much.

    In fact,
    I find nothing at all.

I swear Mahmoud I hear your voice now. I am not imagining it. Your voice like the overhead speaker reciting the children's names.

A Nakba Museum marks an era that begins in

or 2012 or 2008 or 2006 or 2000 or 1991 or 1987 or 1982 or 1973

or 1967 or 1956 or 1948 or 1947 or 1936 or 1932 or 1929 or 1924

or 1922 or 1919 or 1917 or 1914 or 1904 or 1897 or 1882 or

and ends in

If we are given access beyond the walls
have we entered a museum.
If we live in settlements
are we residing in a museum.
If we live in refugee camps
are we part of a museum.
If we drive on those roads
do we easily access a museum.
If we cross checkpoints and barriers
have we made our way to a museum.
If we are granted permits
can we enter a museum.
If there are no curfews
can we leave a museum.

If the Nakba is still in progress
can we visit a museum.

Mahmoud,
Forgive me:

> but I now picture us
> sitting in a café in a museum.
> Specifically, the United States
> Holocaust Memorial Museum.

I imagine you debating between the Tuna with Havarti Dill
Cheese and the Smoked Salmon Caesar Wrap.

I order the Spinach, Brie and Pear on Walnut Raisin Bread.

> I imagine your insistence on paying
> but I have a student discount
> and I pay.

> I can be stubborn like that.

We sit silently in the museum, contemplating about what we have seen, what it means, and how we continue to live our lives as if these people are mere shadows or images hanging on the walls. Their names are like other names. Like other annihilations. We do not want to talk about what it means for a group of people to die intentionally, as if dying is the purpose of living. We do not want to look into each other's eyes because then we would have to share the embarrassment of not knowing the answers or of asking more questions and we are both so tired so tired so damn tired of asking questions.

We examine the dessert options: Fresh Fruit Cup, Fruit Smoothie, Ice Cream, Cheesecake, Brownie, Jumbo Cookie, Chips, or Granola Bar.

We would rather discuss dessert. It is much easier.

I respond: "The cheesecake sounds good,
                    but I am willing to compromise."

We continue talking but we know that every word actually conceals what has not been said or what we would rather not say because, the truth is, asking for directions to a museum that does not exist might call upon its very existence.

Museums create histories through artifacts.
Museums transform objects into units of time.
Museums dispossess possessions.
Museums are battles over memory.
Museums are systematically planned.
Museums remind us how
violently we are born.

Museums reflect our origins
emerging from the burden of a past.

We enter a museum with sadness
and relief
because we are alive
in our moments of observation
and are confronted with
our own existence
hardly seeing the distance between
our bodies and the artifacts.

We then walk away from   those lives
those people
those histories.

To leave on our own accord is a privilege.

You and I would rather not call things by the names they inherit.

A person's death – whether through murder or cleansing or rape
or suicide or gas or fire or water or glass or air or brick or stone
or age or disease or weapon or accident or assault or bite or fall
or kick or rope or strangulation or smoke or heat or nature or
food or alcohol or poison – is a death.

A death is a death.

And a museum: a failure
to commemorate
the most direct possible expression.

Afterthoughts

Like many Israelis, I had little/no access to Palestinian literature. I discovered Mahmoud Darwish by mere chance in the late 1990s between the pages of the anthology *Victims of a Map* in a used-books store in Tel Aviv. I was intrigued by the title but also surprised to learn about a writer whose "first collection of poetry was published in 1960, and since then…has become perhaps the best-known Palestinian poet in the world." I set out to locate additional books but could only find Darwish's *The Music of Human Flesh*.

Mahmoud Darwish struggled against being/becoming a representative of the Palestinian people. *Dear Darwish* enables me to encounter him as a poet whose existence was denied to me.

I encounter him as a voice from "the other side," a voice so threatening to Israeli society that when former Minister of Education Yossi Sarid tried to add two of Darwish's apolitical poems in the educational curriculum, the initiative caused enough controversy that right wing Knesset members released a motion of no confidence. The poems never made it in. Although Darwish's poetry is celebrated around the world, many Jewish-Israelis are still oblivious to his writing, political activism, and international acclaim.

The sparks that ignited the essence of this project were set in late 2008 after Israel's attacks in the Gaza Strip. I recall, most vividly, driving my scooter down *HaShalom* St. in Tel Aviv and seeing a group of protesters supporting what later became "Operation Cast Lead." Signs were erected on street corners blaring, "Israel has a right to protect itself." At first, I instinctively related to that message; but as I drove home something felt wrong, though I couldn't understand or articulate the nature of that "thing" at that particular moment.

When I moved back to the U.S. in the summer of 2009, the seams of the blindfolds I was forced to wear in Israel loosened. My growing feeling of discomfort gradually manifested into a new political reality. This project traces that process.

Notes

Pg. 17-19: This first piece, of what would later become *Dear Darwish*, was written several days after the "prisoner swap" between Israel and Hamas on October 18, 2011. Gilad Shalit, an Israel Defense Forces (IDF) solider, was released *in exchange* for 1,027 prisoners. The negotiations received international attention and support. However, Israeli society was divided, as many claimed that hundreds of Palestinian prisoners had "blood on their hands," i.e. were involved in acts of terror against Israeli targets and civilians. Aziz Salha, one of the prisoners released in this exchange, participated in the 2000 Ramallah lynching during the Second Intifada. He was photographed displaying his blood-stained hands to a cheering crowd, following the killing and dismemberment of two IDF reservists.

The poem invokes excerpts from Mahmoud Darwish, "Who Am I, Without Exile?" *The Butterfly's Burden*, trans. Fady Joudah (Port Townsend: Copper Canyon Press, 2007), 88-91; Rachel Zolf, "Day Four" in "L'éveil," *Neighbour Procedure* (Toronto: Coach House Books, 2010), 78; Jack Spicer, "Berkeley in Time of Plague" and *After Lorca* in *My Vocabulary Did This to Me: The Collected Poetry of Jack Spicer*, eds. Peter Gizzi and Kevin Killian (Middletown: Wesleyan University Press, 2008), 5, 110-111.

Pg. 20: Since early 2000, thousands of Palestinian minors, under the legal age of "criminal responsibility," have been illegally arrested, detained, and/or imprisoned by Israeli authorities.

Pg. 23: The reference appears in Julia Cameron, *The Artist's Way* (Jeremy P. Tarcher/Putnam: New York, 1992), 68.

Pg. 27: The last line was borrowed from the website *ChaCha* in answer to the question "How much pain can a person stand before dying?" See: http://www.chacha.com/question/how-much-pain-can-a-person-stand-before-dying

Pg. 37: The poem includes excerpts from David Antin, "tuning," *Tuning* (New Directions: New York, 1984), 139-140.

Pg. 39-40: This piece interweaves references from Mahmoud Darwish, *In the Presence of Absence* (Archipelago Books: Brooklyn, 2011), 16-17, 34.

Pg. 43-44: The poem references definitions of "to" and Spicer, *After Lorca*, 108-109, 111. Spicer employs (mis)translations of Lorca's poetry and often invokes the late poet's "voice" in the form of prose letters. See: "to" *Merriam-Webster.com*, Merriam-Webster, http://www.merriam-webster.com/dictionary/to

Pg. 45: "The echo has no echo" employs Mahmoud Darwish, "The girl/The scream," *A River Dies of Thirst*, trans. Catherine Cobham (Archipelago Books: Brooklyn, 2009), 3.

Pg. 46: "That anger there sitting packed up neatly" was written in response to an article about Nazi soldiers raping Jewish women during the Holocaust. I discovered this essay while researching rape crimes committed by Jewish soldiers against Palestinian women before, during, and after the Nakba.
See: Jessica Ravitz, "Silence Lifted: The Untold Stories of Rape during the Holocaust," *CNN.com*, CNN, published June 24, 2011,http://www.cnn.com/2011/WORLD/europe/06/24/holocaust.rape/

Pg. 47: "Plan D" is a reference to "Plan Dalet:" the strategic, systematic, and planned expulsion of Palestinians by Jews in Mandatory British Palestine in 1948. See: Ilan Pappé, *The Ethnic Cleansing of Palestine* (Oneworld Publications: Oxford, 2006).

Pg. 48-49: "סְלִיחָה" (*Slicha*) translates as forgiveness, pardon, and atonement in Hebrew. It is also an expression for: "I'm sorry," "Excuse me" or "Pardon me."

Pg. 50-51: "After *Yom Kippur*" alludes to the Day of Atonement, the holiest day of the Jewish calendar occurring during the Tenth day of Tishri, the seventh month of the Hebrew year. The piece evokes Leviticus 16 and 23 and various *Viddui* (confession) prayers. The Jewish confession prayer *Ashamnu* ("We have sinned"), or *Viddui Katan* (the "abbreviated confession"), has been reappropriated and intentionally mistranslated to English.

Pg. 53-54: The poem references Spicer, *After Lorca*, 123.

Pg. 59-78 "After November 29" alludes to Psalm 34.15, as well as the 1947 United Nations Partition Plan for Palestine and the 2012 United Nations General Assembly Resolution 67/19. The text reappropriates speeches delivered by Palestinian President Mahmoud Abbas and Israeli UN Ambassador Ron Prosor on November 29, 2012. Italicized words signify borrowed text from both speeches; President Abbas's speech appears in bold. While representatives from 138 countries approved the resolution to grant Palestine a non-member observer state status in the UN, nine countries rejected it, including Israel and the U.S.

See: Mahmoud Abbas, "Address to UN General Assembly," *TimesofIsrael.com*, Times of Israel, (speech, New York, NY, November 29, 2012), http://www.timesofisrael.com/full-text-of-mahmoud-abbass-speech-to-the-un-general-assembly-november-29-2012/; Ron Prosor, "Address to UN General Assembly," *TimesofIsrael.com*, Times of Israel, (speech, New York, NY, November 29, 2012), http://www.timesofisrael.com/full-text-of-ron-prosors-speech-to-the-un-general-assembly-november-29-2012/

Pg. 81-103: The Nakba, meaning "catastrophe" or "disaster" in Arabic, refers to the expulsion and displacement of over 700,000 Palestinians beginning in 1947; the term is often synonymous with the period that marks the Israeli War of Independence.

"Nakba Museum" references or extracts words, sentences, and phrases from *Nakba: Palestine, 1948, and the Claims of Memory*, eds. Ahmad H. Sa'di and Lila Abu-Lughod (Columbia University Press: New York, 2007); C.D. Wright, "Not the mental lethargy in which the days enveloped her," *One With Others* (Cooper Canyon Press: Port Townsend, 2011), 140-141; Wikipedia contributors, "List of Holocaust Memorials and Museums," *Wikipedia*, The Free Encyclopedia, http://en.wikipedia.org/wiki/List_of_Holocaust_memorials_and_museums; Museum Café, United States Holocaust Memorial Museum, http://www.ushmm.org/information/museum-cafe.

Acknowledgements

This project has been an inseparable part of my life during the last two years. I want to thank you, dear reader, for now sharing this journey with me.

I would also like to thank my dear friends whose comments have helped shape this book: Robin Brox, David Hadbawnik, Emily Anderson, Prabha Manuratne, Melissa Schindler, Roman Filkovsky, Joe Hall, Buddika Bandura, and Dan Madden. Thank you for your thoughtful, insightful, and incredibly significant feedback. Thank you to Know Hope for your permission to use *The Notion of Homeland* for the cover image (painted as part of WALL\THERAPY, Rochester, NY in August 2013).

Thank you to Geoffrey Gatza, editor of BlazeVOX, who heard me read the first "Dear Mahmoud" during the Saucebox Poetry Performance at the 2012 Buffalo Infringement Festival. Since then, your support and encouragement have pushed this project forward, and I sincerely appreciate your patience and generosity.

This project would not be possible without the support and love of my partner, Guy Weiss.

Guy, thank you for believing in me and in my writing. Thank you for attending every poetry reading with a camera at hand. Thank you for always clapping the loudest and longest. Thank you for forcing me to sit down and finish this book. Thank you for constantly uttering words of encouragement, for praising my rough drafts, and for accompanying me for hours on end (even during your days off/post-call days) while I recite, edit, read, reread, write, and rewrite. Thank you for reading almost every single word, line, and draft of this text. Thank you for helping make this book a reality.

תודה רבה אהובי. כל מילה מוקדשת לך.

Morani Kornberg-Weiss was born in Tel Aviv, Israel and spent her early childhood in Southern California. After completing her military service, B.A. in Psychology and English, and the beginning of her graduate degree in Israel, she moved to Buffalo, NY to pursue a Ph.D. in English at SUNY Buffalo's Poetics Program. Her scholarship revolves around the Israeli-Palestinian conflict and the lyric tradition. Her poetry has been published in multiple venues including *The Last Stanza, Voices Israel, Genius Floored, Omnia Vanitas Review, kadar koli, eccolinguistics*, and *arc*. Her Hebrew translation of Karen Alkalay-Gut's *Miracles & More* was published by Keshev in 2012. She currently lives in Los Angeles, CA with her partner, two cats, dog, and a lentil.